Miss Quinn's farm

T0372087

Mum and I are off to Miss Quinn's. She has a farm not far out of town.

Mum turns into the farm.
We can see Miss Quinn. She
seems to be in a bit of a rush.

5

We look for the sheep
with Miss Quinn.

7

We see cows on the
hill, but no sheep.

We see a barn
owl napping.

We see the hens in the
coop sitting on eggs.

The ducks are down by
the dam. But the sheep
are not in sight.

I run to check the goat pen.
A big goat and her kids are
out of the goat pen.

And I can see sheep **in** the goat pen! I yell to Mum and Miss Quinn.

15

Words to blend

farm	far	barn
turns	napping	seems
need	rush	sheep
shut	right	sight
might	look	happen
sitting	coop	check
goat	missing	Quinn

Before reading

Synopsis: Mum and Dan visit Miss Quinn on her farm. She is in a rush to find her sheep, so they go to help her.

Review graphemes/phonemes: ar or ur

New grapheme/phoneme: ow

Story discussion: Look at the cover and read the title together. Ask: *Who do you think the person on the cover is?* (Miss Quinn) *How do you think she's feeling?* (She looks quite worried.) Ask children what they think will happen in the story. Why might the farmer, Miss Quinn, be looking worried?

Link to prior learning: Display the grapheme *ow*. Say: *These two letters are a digraph – that means they make one sound.* Write or display these words: *town, owl, howl, now*. How quickly can children identify the *ow* grapheme and read the words?

Vocabulary check: coop – a house for chickens; pen – an enclosure for animals such as sheep

Decoding practice: Display the word *napping*. Check that children can split it into syllables (n-a-pp/i-ng). Can they sound out and blend the sounds in each syllable to read the word?

Tricky word practice: Display the word *by* and ask children to circle the tricky part of the word *(y, which makes an /igh/ sound)*. Practise writing and reading this word.

After reading

Apply learning: Ask: *Can you sum up this story in just one or two sentences?* (e.g. Mum and Dan help Miss Good to find her missing sheep. The goats have got out of their pen, and the sheep have got in.)

Comprehension

- What problem did Miss Quinn have?
- How did the sheep get into the goat pen?
- What animals were on the hill?

Fluency

- Pick a page that most of the group read quite easily. Ask them to reread it with pace and expression. Model how to do this if necessary.
- Ask children to turn to pages 6–7 and read the speech bubbles with lots of expression.
- Practise reading the words on page 17.

Tricky words review

and	your	she
out	into	we
to	be	you
no	my	by
her	for	all